INDIAN ENCHANTMENT

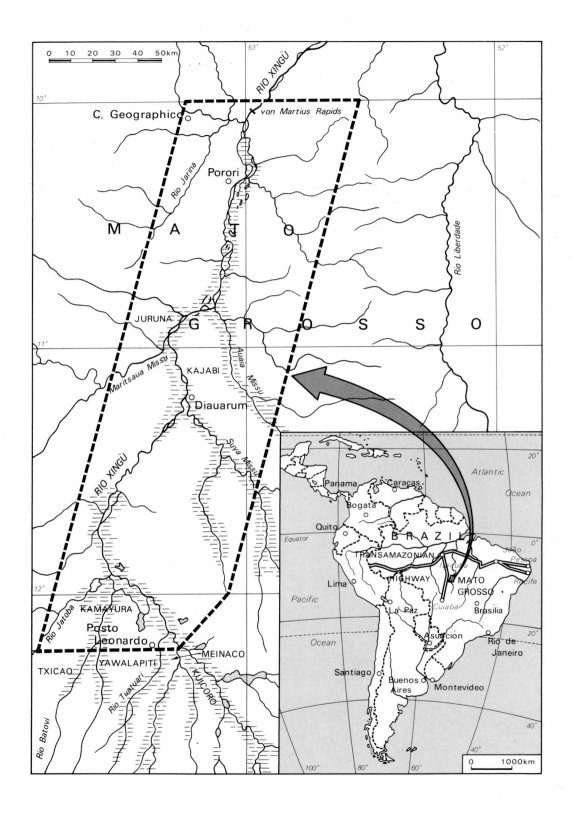

LEOPOLD OF BELGIUM

INDIAN ENCHANTMENT

Memories of a sojourn among the Indians of the Upper-Xingù

Gateway Publishers Inc., Los Angeles

EDITOR'S NOTE

Since this book was written and the photographs which constitute the body of this work were gathered together, the face of Brazil has changed profoundly, most notably following the development of a road network. The region of the Upper Xingù, previously protected by distance and isolation, saw its integrity threatened. Undoubtedly indispensible to the economic growth of Brazil, the Transamazonian Highway, which unfortunately traverses the National Park of the Xingù, has brought not only the benefits but also the evils of progress.

Thus, we consider this book one of the last testaments of a primitive civilisation on the way to destruction.

This work is published under the direction of Francis Ambrière with the collaboration of Claude Janicot.

RIO DE JANEIRO, October 10, 1964, 6.00 A.M.: Jean-Pierre Gosse, ichthyologist at the Institute of Natural Sciences of Belgium and myself, met our good friend and pilot, Colonel Camarào, on the airfield of Santos Dumont. Our destination: the sources of the Xingù.

At 5.30 P.M. that same day, after several stops and a flight of about 1250 miles, we landed at Posto Leonardo. The excellent runway here is only one of the many the Brazilian Air Force has built, even in the remotest areas of Brazil, inaccessible by any other means.

And what a contrast! People, sites, customs, everything was new.

The three brothers of the Villas-Boas family, Orlando, Claudio and Alvaro, welcomed us with open arms. These three men, who are responsible for the protection of the Indians of the Upper Xingù, were surrounded by their fellow workers and by the Indian population of the post. The Indians were of various tribes, completely naked, and as curious to see us as we were to see them.

It is an extraordinary moment when men of two different worlds meet face to face: it is only a moment because the shock of the encounter disappears almost immediately. It is astonishing how easily we can, in a few seconds, adapt ourselves to such a radical change of way of life and accept, without the least surprise, scenes and morals far removed from those we are accustomed to. I have experienced this same phenomenon in other encounters with the primitive populations of Africa, Asia, Indonesia, as well as in tropical America. The sensation of losing one's bearings is more intuitive than physical. It is, at the same time, a reaching back to the fundamental truths hidden in our nature and gives us a deep feeling of brotherhood with all men, no matter what origin, belief, or civilisation.

What is Posto Leonardo?

This village owes its name to the eldest of the Villas-Boas brothers, who died a short time ago. He, like his three brothers, Orlando, Claudio and Alvaro, devoted his entire life to the protection of the Indians. Posto Leonardo serves as the administrative base of the National Park of the Upper Xingù and owes its fairly recent establishment, in 1961, to the efforts of dedicated workers during several generations.

Explorations did not begin until the end of the nineteenth century. Natural barriers protected the region of the Upper Xingù from any penetration; in the south there are the high plateaux of the Mato Grosso, and in the north a series of tumultuous rapids make navigation impossible. Thus the 1250 mile long Xingù river, which flows from a group of smaller rivers whose source is near the watershed of the Amazon and Paraguay, has been the least explored of the Amazon's tributaries.

In 1884, however, the German explorer, Karl von Steinen, with a detachment from the Brazilian Imperial Army, left Cuiabá, the capital of Mato Grosso, to explore and chart the Xingù. In 1896 and 1899, Meyer and Dr. Karl Ranke followed their fellow-countryman's route. But the Upper Xingù soon became very treacherous. About 1900, five Americans were massacred by the Suya Indians. In 1925, Colonel Fawcett mysteriously disappeared with his party and ten years later, Albert de Winton, the American journalist, was murdered.

In spite of the bravery of these pioneers and the information which they collected, the Upper Xingù was still remarkably isolated until the end of the First World War. At that time, the progress of aviation provided the means to overcome the obstacles of the rivers and jungle: the white man could approach the Indian tribes, which, until then, had been able to preserve their primitive culture and live like men of the Stone Age.

From as ethnological point of view, the reports of these explorations provided valuable knowledge of the Indians of the Xingù. Four linguistic families are to be found in the region: the Karibe, the Aruak, the Tupi and the Yê. To these, two isolated groups should be added: the Trumaï and the Juruna.

Karl von Steinen observed a certain cultural unity among all these tribes, a sign of a fairly long history of coexistence. In spite of different origins, through barter, marriages between the villages and other contacts between the tribes, their way of life has become more uniform. So it is difficult, today, to attribute to any one Indian group a particular form of culture. Some of the characteristics common to the tribes of the Upper Xingù are the structure of the village and its dwellings, the intensive use of manioc and a preference for fish; and very remarkably, the total absence of alcoholic drink among all the tribes.

Even though the Indians do not know how to weave, they can braid the fiber of wild cotton or the muriti palm for hammocks, headbands and armbands.

Among the Aruak groups, the art of pottery is a speciality, and these products are exchanged for those of other tribes. For sport, wrestling matches, called *huca-huca*, are popular, as well as dances, some of which require the wearing of wood or straw masks.

Though contacts with the exterior world have multiplied since the first explorations, the Indians ancestral way of life has been modified very little. It is true that certain tribes now know the use of firearms; aluminium and iron household utensils have replaced some made of stone or earthenware, and the system of barter has changed somewhat.

But these factors have not changed their fundamental way of life. Alas, this does not mean that these contacts with the outside world had no effect on the Indians. On the contrary, external influences rapidly threatened the moral and physical health of the population—even the very existence of the tribes. In 1896, Dr. Ranke had already given a warning that the explorations would introduce pathogenic germs into the region, against which the Indians were not immunized. In fact, in the years that followed, epidemics such as influenza and measles caused many deaths.

When permanent posts, and later, air bases were established the workers and soldiers living there soon introduced another problem; venereal diseases, until then unknown, had terrible effects.

In 1918, the deadly Spanish flu spread to Brazil; in the Xingù region several villages were wiped out. In 1946, a new influenza epidemic again caused many deaths.

A comparison between the population figures of 1884 and those of 1952 shows a striking decrease in population. In 1884, there were thirty-nine villages and 3,000 people. In 1952, there were only ten villages and 650 people, a decrease of nearly 80 percent in a little over sixty years!

Fortunately, a few far-seeing men realized that the very survival of the

Indian tribes was threatened and succeeded in gaining official support from the Brazilian government for their protection, before it was too late.

One of the first of these was the famous Colonel Rondon, who drew up a complete plan for the protection of the Indians. With a strong personality, great charm and inspired by humanitarian ideals and an interest in ethnology, Rondon saw the importance and the urgency of the task and devoted his life to it. With amazing endurance, he travelled thousands of miles across the terrifying Brazilian jungle, on foot, on horseback and by canoe.

Under his impetus, the Brazilian government created the Service for the Protection of the Indians, whose role was not only to protect them from intrusion but also to give them medical help and social assistance and to safeguard their culture from the encroachments of civilisation. Rondon, whose motto was "Rather die than kill an Indian", has become a legendary figure over there.

The Villas-Boas brothers have been worthy successors of Colonel Rondon; in 1946 they led a difficult and important mission known as the "Roncador-Xingù Expedition". Inspired by the same high ideals, they too, have devoted their lives to ensuring the survival of the primitive peoples. On their initiative, in 1952, a commission of specialists proposed to the National Congress the rough draft of a law to create a reserve for the Indians of the Xingù where no private property would be allowed. But it was not until 1961, by a decree of the President of the Brazilian Republic, that the National Park of the Upper Xingù was created, in a territory about the size of Belgium.

The Villas-Boas brothers administer this area as officials of the federal government, but in an independent and autonomous manner. Their aims are to ensure the survival of the Indians, if possible to give them a new impetus and to shelter them from disrupting contact with a civilisation so different from theirs. If these essential goals can be achieved, the time will come later to consider other aspects of the development of the Indians. There have already been encouraging results for the future. Between 1952 and 1963, in spite of serious epidemics and other unfavorable factors, the population of the Upper Xingù has been maintained. Compare this with the disastrous decline in population between 1884 and 1952 and it is clear that the measures taken by Rondon, the Villas-Boas brothers and the Brazilian government are the right ones.

———————————————

This, then, was the situation in the Upper Xingù ten years ago, when Jean-Pierre Gosse and I arrived—a reserve vigilantly defended against the influx of men or disease by a team of pioneers.

10

After the eldest of the Villas-Boas brothers died, the three remaining ones divided up the work. Posto Leonardo became the main residence of Orlando, who administers the National Park with the help of Claudio. To cover a wider area, Claudio is stationed at Diauarum, the post he founded. Alvaro, the youngest of the three brothers, is in charge of "public relations".

Posto Leonardo is the link between the National Park and the white man's world. Once a week, the C. A. N. plane which flies from Rio to Manaos supplies the post with food, medicine and other necessary provisions, brings mail and evacuates the sick or injured.

Indians of neighboring tribes often visit the post, and little by little, some of them have decided to stay. Thus, Posto Leonardo is not an ordinary Indian village; it is a somewhat artificial centre that attracts, by its air-link with "civilisation", the Meinaco, Yawalapiti, Kamayura, etc.

Two small planes and canoes with outboard motors are at the disposal of the Villas-Boas brothers and members of scientific missions who stay in the region. With the use of these, my companions and myself were able to visit true Indian villages, sleeping with the natives in their large huts and sharing in their way of life.

The Indian huts are very large and can house several families. Made in elliptical form, they are covered with *sapé* grass, with the roof and sides in one continuous line. Each long side has a very small opening in order to keep the inside of the hut as cool as possible; to enter the hut one must nearly bend double.

The huts in each village are built in a circle, freeing a large area in the middle for two special constructions. First, a large hut which serves for meetings and ceremonies; this is generally called the "House of Flutes", undoubtedly because the flute players and men of the tribe assemble there for certain solemn rituals. Secondly, there is a large conical cage, made of long poles gathered together at the top. It houses an eagle to which the inhabitants of the village bring quantities of food. Does this eagle represent the protective spirit of the village?

I do not know, but it plays some role in the mystical life of the Indians.

For obvious reasons (fishing and travelling by canoe), the villages are always located near the water. But, for safety, they are built a certain distance away into the forest. A footpath, well camouflaged by the luxuriant vegetation, leads from the river to the village and ends in front of the chief's hut.

Day after day, Indian life follows the same peaceful rhythm. The men may hunt or fish, construct or repair huts, take part in assemblies that look

11

after their common interests, or keep fit, by taking part in such sports as archery or the wrestling called *huca-huca*. The women, as in all primitive societies, do the domestic work: they take care of the children, prepare the meals, press the manioc, prepare the thin cakes and cut wood for the fire. They grow the manioc, sugar cane, banana trees, rice, beans, papayas and pineapples. . . .

The day invariably closes with a wonderful swim in a nearby river; here children and adults shout and play joyfully together, forgetting their tiredness and the heat of the day.

Fishing, like hunting, is practised with large bows, and arrows of *huba* wood with feathers stitched to each side.

The only native means of transport is the canoe, made of *jatoba* bark or hollowed out of a tree trunk and propelled by long paddles with parallel sides. Clothing is unknown. Men and women paint their bodies extensively and use many ornaments; shell necklaces (or glass beads for some of the tribes who have had contact with the outside world); headdresses made of brightly colored feathers; armbands, wrist, leg and ankle bracelets made of braided fibers; sometimes the women wear a small bark loin cloth. This is their entire clothing.

The art of weaving is unknown in the Upper Xingù. Only braiding is used; fiber and bark are the principal materials in making certain utensils, sacks for pressing the manioc, hammocks and some ornaments and bands.

The only objects that can be termed "furniture" are the curious stools, carved from a single block of wood, often in the form of animals.

The art of pottery is mainly of Aruak origin and consists of household items, pots and vases of various sizes, whose shapes are often of animal form, like the stools. Generally, the pieces of pottery have a black interior while the exterior has a simple red coating or a linear design.

For recreation, besides archery and the *huca-huca*, there are dances, separate ones for men and women, some of which entail the wearing of curious masks. These must have some mystical significance.

One particularly torrid afternoon, when we were swinging in our hammocks to try to break up the air, Orlando proposed a "Round Table" conference, seated in the lukewarm waters of the Tuatuari, the river, hardly twenty yards wide, which flows past Posto Leonardo.

"For a long time", he said, "I have heard about a certain tribe called the Txicào, which is located somewhere on the banks of the Rio Batovi, not far from the southern limits of the National Park. These Txicào have the reputation of being a particularly wild tribe; they hold themselves apart from the other tribes and no one knows their language".

"It would be exciting", Orlando continued, "to make contact with these mysterious Txicào. Although the rains have returned, shall we risk an attempt? The operation would be in two phases: one, or possibly more, air reconnaissances to find the exact location of the Indians and the possibilities of landing; then the landing and making contact with them".

Orlando then invited me on this "Operation Pacification", as he called it. I accepted with enthusiasm.

We reconnoitred the area without difficulty. After twenty minutes' flight, in our Cessna piloted by Genario Gomèz, the famous jungle pilot, we reached Rio Batovi. No habitation was visible. After an hour's flight over the region, we flew over a winding river which, as far as we could judge, must have been the Rio Jatoba; we flew very low, skimming over the tops of the trees. Suddenly we saw, at a bend in the river, on the brilliant white sand, five Indians running as fast as they could go to the refuge of the forest, their bodies dripping with water; astonished by the sight of our plane, they must have left their bathing very hastily. We were filled with delight—we had just seen our first Txicào. Then a few moments later, we saw a large hut with several Indians around it. Here in this area were at least some of the people we were looking for.

On a second air reconnaissance of the region, we discovered a possible landing spot quite near the large hut we had located previously. In this clearing, we dropped pieces of cloth and other objects, to convince our future hosts of our friendly intentions.

But our plans for coming again and landing were stopped abruptly by a series of stormy days that were probably transforming our clearing into an impassable swamp. Luckily several days later, the weather cleared, and one beautiful morning, we decided to begin our venture, taking two planes. The "Spirit of Philadelphia", our first plane, took the Villas-Boas brothers. This plane, and its pilot, Tim, belonged to the Summer Institute of Linguistics. Genario was the pilot of the second plane, the Cessna, taking Professor Galvão, the distinguished anthropologist of the University of Brasília, the cameraman and myself.

The weather became worse again in the course of our flight. Great dark clouds hovered just above the forest, and we had to fly at a very low altitude. Fortunately the rain we feared held off and we soon found our clearing.

After circling round the area several times, the "Spirit of Philadelphia" made a good landing. Genario landed his Cessna with the same skill, proving what able pilots we had.

As soon as we landed, naked men suddenly appeared out of their hiding-places from all parts of the forest. Armed with bows and arrows, they grinned nervously at us.

About a hundred yards separated us from the Txicào. They stood quite still and we stayed there, motionless, looking at each other. They seemed smaller, less robust and lighter-skinned than the other inhabitants of the Upper Xingù. At last, two of them grew bold and came towards us. They went first to Orlando, whom they touched timidly. He gave them some smaller objects we had brought for this purpose. Then the others approached, vying with each other to offer us necklaces, charms and small baskets they had made. As for any verbal communication . . . without a single word in common, Indians and whites could only stare at each other curiously.

When we were ready to leave, having cleared and leveled our landing site as best we could with hoes, a young Txicào followed us. He entered the "Spirit of Philadelphia" of his own free will, driven no doubt by intense curiosity. Orlando jumped at the opportunity to take a representative of the Txicào with us, to show him Posto Leonardo and the Indians of other tribes.

This would be a great step forward in the integration of the Txicào in the National Park. But though this young man had entered the plane of his own accord, his boldness left him when the door closed and the engine started. Seated next to me, he buried his head under my arm and his whole body trembled. After several minutes, he recovered a little; I persuaded him to look out of the cabin window. Looking at the world from this new angle interested him so much, he forget his fears.

Soon we landed at Posto Leonardo. Orlando toured the post with this young Txicào and introduced him to the other Indians who thronged round with curiosity. Though very nervous, he faced this situation with courage and even forced himself to smile. Soon afterwards, our reluctant tourist was flown back to his own people.

Thus ended a very memorable day.

———————————

Diauarum, from an Indian word meaning "black jaguar", is a post created on the banks of the Xingù, about twenty years ago, by Claudio Villas-Boas. It is not an ordinary Indian village. Like Posto Leonardo, Indians from different tribes in the area live there: Suya, Trumaï, Kajabi, Juruna . . .

Hidden under green palms, Diauarum overlooks the river Xingù, already several hundreds of yards wide, flowing smoothly and silently towards the distant Amazon. As it penetrates further north, the savanna characteristic of the area around Posto Leonardo is gradually replaced by dense tropical forest; the trees are covered with thick creepers, so closely interwoven that they make the banks impenetrable.

After fishing for several days in small rivers and nearby lagoons, we continued our course down the Xingù. When we could, we spent the night in an Indian village near the river, or if there was no village, we hung our hammocks in the open wherever we happened to be when night fell.

We were able to spend an evening and stay the night with the famous Juruna, or rather, the last fifty representatives of this tribe, which was once the most powerful in Brazil. These Indians have striking features, fine noses and shoulder-length hair. Bibina, their leader, who had a small greying beard, understood Portuguese and was very attached to Claudio. He gave us a friendly welcome, offering us fresh fish, bananas, mangos, pineapples and a forest fruit the Indians call *piki*. The size of a small mango the *piki* has an enormous stone surrounded by rich, nourishing, yellow flesh.

The next evening we were the guests of a new tribe, the Txucaramaï, also called the Mecrononti. Their village on the Xingù is named "Porori", meaning "red earth". If the huts here are not as large and imposing as those near Posto Leonardo, the Indians themselves are remarkably tall. Some of the men wear a wooden disk in the lower lip and all have shoulder-length hair. The heads of the women and girls, on the other hand, are almost entirely shaven.

Night fell. An unusually full moon slowly rose in the sky filled with stars. Not a leaf stirred. The heat was suffocating. In the village, men and women danced, in separate groups facing each other. Two tall Indians, taking me by the arm, invited me to dance with their group—two steps forward, then two steps back, keeping in time with a highly rhythmic but monotonous tune. As I took part in this dance, I let my imagination wander. Was I really there, in this fabulous place, among men of another age, or was it all a dream?

Lightning suddenly lit up the horizon and rolls of thunder broke the silence of the peaceful valley of the Xingù. The dancing ended. Late at night, when the storm broke and torrents of rain plunged down, I lay in my hammock re-living this extraordinary day.

At sunrise, Kremuro, chief of the village, invited us to stay and see the arrival of a group of about 150 Txucaramaï, who were coming from the river Iriri, a distance of two or three hundred miles. We did not want to miss this

15

event. But we had just enough time to go to the von Martius rapids first. The rapids mark the northern border of the National Park as well as the border between the states of Mato Grosso and Pará.

After a long journey by canoe, we made camp at the start of the rapids. No human being can live in this region for long, due to the insects of all kinds and sizes, whose bites and stings are nearly unbearable. The rapids, stretching for about ten miles and blocking the river completely, are named after the famous German botanist, von Martius, who described the flora of Brazil in the eighteenth century.

We spent two or three days there, fishing among the rocks, the rapids and the whirlpools. Then we returned to Porori, where the tribe from the Iriri soon arrived.

I will never forget the sight of the arrival of this group of men, women and children, exhausted by weeks of walking through the dark, hostile jungle. Kremuro, chief of Porori, came forward to meet Kretire, the chief of the newcomers. They embraced and, for some time, shed tears in a most mournful way. This, it seems, is the traditional ceremony which takes place when two friendly tribes meet.

These new arrivals lost no time in beginning the construction of their small huts, evidently temporary, but nevertheless carefully covered, because the rainy season had begun.

I watched, impressed by the skill and speed with which these men worked, choosing and cutting the stakes and branches of the palm tree, and stripping the bark with which to bind the construction together. The forest provides for every need.

The next day, the Indians had a surprise planned for us. In scattered groups among the trees, they began to dress and paint themselves. Dressing up, for them, is only a figure of speech: feathers on their heads, bands round the biceps and below the knees, that is all. In making themselves up, they use a red dye (urucú) and a black dye (*genipapo*) on their faces in freakish designs that change for each festival. These preparations made, we were treated to a marvelously colored and animated spectacle. Indifferent to the torrid heat, the Indians began a frenzied dance, savage rather than graceful, to the rhythm of a strange chant interspersed with raucous cries. By means of these chants and dances, the Indians wanted to show us that they accepted our being among them. One of the Txucaramaï particularly attracted my attention. Long hair surrounded his impassive face; his look fascinated me. He was called Kobroti and had the reputation of having magical powers over snakes. He willingly ac-

16

companied me when I went into the forest. His manner, kindly and dignified but mysterious as well, made him appear to me the very image of the Indian I had dreamt about since early childhood, majestic and secret.

We really regretted leaving Porori and its inhabitants, the Mecrononti, until only recently the most feared of the Cayapo Indians.

One evening, returning to Diauarum, we decided to stop for the night in a sheltered place high on the right bank of the Xingù. While some of us set up camp and prepared the fire, others hunted for duck in a nearby lagoon; two magnificent birds rewarded their efforts. After a long and hard day's canoeing, the sight of these ducks on the spit made everyone cheerful.

But alas! Suddenly the sky grew dark and torrents of water, driven by a violent wind, beat down on us. Drenched to the bone, we had to abandon the modest feast we had looked forward to so much.

We had hoped to refresh ourselves, but with our remaining stocks of *cachassa*, not with rainwater.

That night was wet and disagreeable. In this deluge, only the toads seemed happy as they treated us to an unmelodious and deafening concert.

We re-visited the village of the Juruna, finally arriving in Diauarum late at night. We stayed here two weeks longer, exploring the surrounding country.

Of the visits we made among the different Indian groups in this region, the most interesting was our stay among the Suya, who live on the banks of the Suya Missu, a tributary of the Xingù.

Like the Juruna, the Suya Indians are a proud people and until the last few years were fiercely hostile to any foreign interference. They were responsible, in the past, for the murder of numerous whites. Their physical appearance has much in common with the Juruna. Men and women have aquiline noses and lovely long black hair, which falls to their shoulders. Like the Txucaramaï, some men wear a labial disk in their lower lip. It is a beautiful and haughty race.

But the time came to leave the National Park of the Upper Xingù and its fascinating inhabitants. I had to rejoin the modern world . . .

Flying back to civilisation in a DC-3 of the Brazilian Air Force, memories of the past weeks kept coming into my mind. I found it hard to leave these places where I had experienced so much, and where I had become so deeply and sincerely attached to the peoples that remind us so strongly of the first ages of man.

These Indians have a striking appearance, an alert and penetrating expression, reflecting the mystery of the great forest.

Robust, healthy, well proportioned, they look magnificent; they have natural grace and pride. Their whole demeanour testifies to their love of life. They frequently embrace each other, a sign of their great need of affection. Inhabiting a country without frontiers, the very size of which excludes any idea of individual ownership, these men and women have a much less petty and egoistic view of life than ourselves. Their behaviour is always completely natural in every situation, a clear sign of their fundamental innocence. Naked and with no personal possessions, they do not know evil or theft and therefore have nothing to hide.

In this age and society, where men are dominated by material preoccupations and their lives, passed in a pointless turmoil, are full of restraints and prejudices, should we not reflect on the simplicity and happiness of these primitive people? It is in thinking of them and in thinking of us that I have chosen the pictures for this book, which bears striking witness to what I would call "Indian Enchantment". The part that I played in this open, spontaneous and enchanted life, with its memory of human kindness in conjunction with the unspoiled beauty of nature, will long remain engraved in my mind and heart.

Léopold
de Belgique.

THE PLATES

1. Young Indian at Posto Leonardo.

2. Arrival of a C.A.N. plane which brings supplies each week to Posto Leonardo (line from Rio to Manaus).

3. A couple from the Yawalapiti tribe with
← their children.

4. Women carrying water by the Rio
   Tuatuari.   →

5. The savanna around Posto Leonardo:
   banks of the Rio Tuatuari.

6—7. Indians of Posto Leonardo. The armbands and belt are made of fiber, the ornaments of feathers. The necklace is made of shells.

8. The family hammock. Yawalapiti Indians. The woman holds a knife given to
← her as a present.

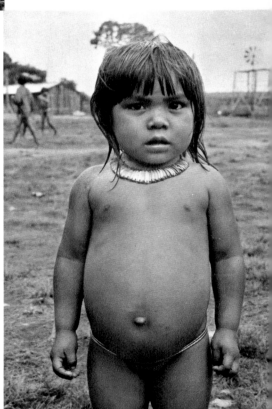

9. A little Yawalapiti girl.
→

← 10. Indians resting in front of their
hut.

11. Child biting into a thin cake made of manioc.
→

13. Familiar scene in front of the village hut.

12. Young woman with a necklace.
←

14. Yawalapiti Indian. Notice the difference between the Indian necklace and the imported glass beads. →

15. Among the Kamayura.
←

16. By the river.
→

17. The guest table at Posto Leonardo. In the background, a portrait of Leonardo Villas-Boas, who gave his name to the post. ←

18. The guest table. The two people in the foreground are the Villas-Boas brothers: Claudio (on the left) and Orlando (on the right).

20. Hacanaï, the young Meinaco who never left the author during his stay.

19. Pizziki.
←

21. An adolescent. Notice the brace-
← lets on the knees and ankles.

22. Fishing with timbo in the Tuatuari
lagoon. Timbo is a vine, the bark of
which contains a poison which has a
paralyzing effect. The Indians make
bundles of sticks from this vine and
beat the water of the lagoon to gather
in the fish which come to the surface.
→

23. J.-P. Gosse holds one
of the containers with fish
destined for the Belgian Institute of Natural Sciences.
←

24. A tame monkey follows the fishing in the lagoon with interest. →

25. Demonstration of archery by Kanato, chief of the ← Yawalapiti tribe.

26. Interior of a Yawalapiti hut. →

27. Lagoon near the village of the Yawalapiti.

28. Among the Yawalapiti.
→

29. *Huca-huca* (wrestling) among
the Kamayura.   →

30. Tacumaï, Kamayura chief, follows
←   a wrestling match with interest.

31. Lagoon near a Kamayura village

32. Inside a Kamayura hut.

33. Kamayura woman.
←

34. Landing of the "Spirit of Philadelphia" in the savanna of the Txicào.　→

35. First contact with the Txicào tribe after the landing. In the center, near the plane, Dr. Galvão, professor of anthropology at the University of Brasília.

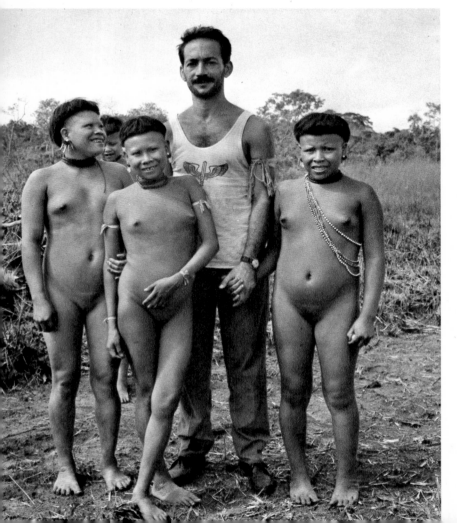

36. Genario Gomèz, the famous jungle pilot,
← surrounded by young Txicào women.

37. Distribution of gifts to the Txicào.
→

38. Orlando Villas-Boas among the Txicào.

39. Txicào Indians. Notice their
   hairstyle.

40. A young Txicào mother and her child. Notice the dried-up bird serving as a charm.

41. Clearing a landing strip. The author at work. →

42. The Villas-Boas brothers distribute presents to the Txicào.

44. The Xingù at Diauarum.

43. Two Trumaï Indians in festival costumes.
←

45—46. Atamaï (on the left), of the Aura tribe, and his friend Aruyavi, of the Trumaï, shooting a fish.

47. Post of Diauarum,
created by Claudio Vil-
las-Boas.

49. Atamaï, an Aura Indian.

48. A blue-eyed Indian: Ahaï of the Trumaï tribe.
←

50. Pepori, Indian of the Kajabi tribe.

51. A Suya Indian woman preparing manioc.

→

52. Atamaï (Aura tribe) and Aruyavi (Trumaï tribe) painted with red and black.

53. A small stream, flowing into the Suya Missu.

55. A lagoon in the forest near the Suya Missu.

54. A Suya Indian in the flooded forest on the banks of the Suya Missu.
←

56. The Xingù
at Diauarum.

57. A fishermen's camp, near the mouth of the Suya Missu. →

58. Kajabi family settled on the banks of the Xingù.

59. Kajabi Indian women weaving

60. Kocumba (Suya tribe) at Diauarum.

61. Passion flower with a coral snake.
→

62. Bibina, chief of the Juruna.

63. A typical Juruna Indian.
→

64. Juruna Indian holding some piranhas
(fish known for their extraordinary voracity).

65. Young Jurunas practising archery.
→

66. Storm on
the Xingù.

67. In the morning haze.

68. The expedition's dugout canoes by the shore of the Xingù where the Jurunas live.

70. Txucaramaï Indian. Notice the way the labial disk is inserted in the lower lip. Only the men observe this custom.

69. Teen-age Juruna.
←

72. Kobroti, of the Txucaramaï tribe, has great power over snakes.

71. Txucaramaï woman crushing manioc.
←

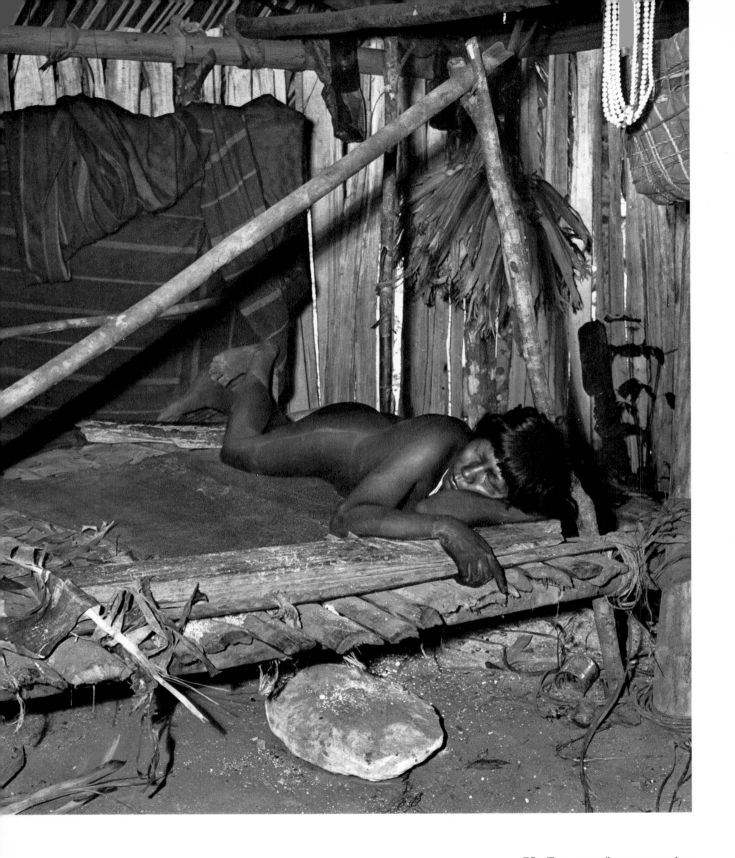

73. Txucaramaï woman resting.

74. Rauni is one of the rare Txucaramaï Indians who speaks some
Portuguese. He served as interpreter.　　　　　→

76. The Rauni family: a mouthful for each.

77. Preparing the fish.

79. Labial disks at their largest size.

81. Txucaramaï women and children at Porori.

80. The animals of the forest share in family life.
←

82. Txucaramaï Indian. His head is decorated with feathers of parrots and other birds of the forest; his face has a mask of red paint. Notice the unusual form of the pipe.

83. A tribe coming from the Rio Iriri has just arrived in Porori, on the banks of the Xingù, to seek the security of the National Park. In accordance with Indian tradition, the chiefs of the two tribes, Kremuro and Kretire, meet each other shedding tears.

84—85. Examples of Txucaramaï make-up.

86. Family meal
in a Txucaramaï
hut.

87—88. Young Txucaramaï people in festival costume.

89. Among the Txucaramaï: grandmother and her grandchildren.

90. In spite of the labial disk, this Txucaramaï can still smoke his pipe.

→

91. Maternal scene among the Txucaramaï.

92. Kobroti has shed his ornaments to go into the forest.

→

93. The hammock is the only comfort in the Indian hut.

94. A family portrait at Porori.

95. The population of Porori watches the expedition pull away.

96. After the hunt: toucan feathers.
→

97. Shade and coolness in the hut.

98. Cattleya orchids abound in the Xingù forest.

99. The formidable piranha is distinguished by its powerful teeth and ← its voracity.

100. Claudio Villas-Boas with the author at the von Martius rapids. These rapids form the northern limits of the Xingù National Park and the boundary between the states of Mato Grosso and Pará. →

101. Bivouac near the von Martius rapids.

102. An Indian of the expedition at rest in his hammock.
        Notice the gun within arm's reach

103. Departure of the fishing expedition to the von Martius rapids.
←

105. At the edge of Lake Yamaricuma in Suya country.

104. The Xingù.
←

106. Example of a Suya Indian.

107. Kuyusi: a Suya chief.

108. Fishing in a stream by Lake Yamaricuma. Notice the sponges in the branches of the trees, which form as a result of flood waters.

109. Interior of a Suya hut.

110. Fishing with the Suya.

111. A lagoon near the mouth of the Suya Missu.

112—113. Work and daily routine among the Suya : the woman makes
bread; the youngster practices archery.

114. Twilight on the Xingù.

LIST OF ILLUSTRATIONS

20. Hacanaï.

21. Adolescent with bracelets.

22. Fishing with timbo in the Tuatuari lagoon.

23. J.-P. Gosse holds one of the containers with fish destined for the Belgian Institute of Natural Sciences.

24. A tame monkey.

25. Demonstration of archery by Kanato.

26. Interior of a Yawalapiti hut.

27. Lagoon near the village of the Yawalapiti.

28. Among the Yawalapiti.

29. *Huca-huca* among the Kamayura.

30. Tacumaï, Kamayura chief, follows a wrestling match with interest.

31. Lagoon near a Kamayura village.

32. Inside a Kamayura hut.

33. Kamayura woman.

34. Landing of the "Spirit of Philadelphia" in the savanna of the Txicào.

35. First contact with the Txicào tribe after the landing.

36. Genario Gomèz, the famous jungle pilot, surrounded by young Txicào women.

37. Distribution of gifts to the Txicào.

38. Orlando Villas-Boas among the Txicào.

39. Txicào Indians.

40. A young Txicào mother and her child.

41. Clearing a landing strip.

42. The Villas-Boas brothers distribute presents to the Txicào.

43. Two Trumaï Indians in festival costumes.

44. The Xingù at Diauarum.

45. Atamaï, of the Aura tribe, prepares to shoot a fish.

46. Aruyavi, of the Trumaï tribe, shooting a fish.

47. The post of Diauarum.

48. A blue-eyed Indian.

49. Atamaï, an Aura Indian.

50. Pepori, Indian of the Kajabi tribe.

51. A Suya Indian woman preparing manioc.

52. Atamaï and Aruyavi painted with red and black.

53. A small stream, flowing into the Suya Missu.

54. A Suya Indian in the flooded forest.

55. A lagoon in the forest near the Suya Missu.

56. The Xingù at Diauarum.

57. A fishermen's camp, near the mouth of the Suya Missu.

58. Kajabi family settled on the banks of the Xingù.

59. Kajabi Indian women weaving.

60. Kocumba (Suya tribe) at Diauarum.

61. Passion flower with a coral snake.

62. Bibina, chief of the Juruna.

63. A typical Juruna Indian.

64. Juruna Indian holding some piranhas.

65. Young Jurunas practising archery.

66. Storm on the Xingù.

67. In the morning haze.

68. The expedition's dugout canoes by the shore of the Xingù where the Jurunas live.

69. Teen-age Juruna.

70. Txucaramaï Indian with a labial disc.

71. Txucaramaï woman crushing manioc.

72. Kobroti, of the Txucaramaï tribe, has great power over snakes.

73. Txucaramaï woman resting.

74. Rauni is one of the rare Txucaramaï Indians who speaks some Portuguese.

75. Txucaramaï men dancing.